The Waterman/Harewood Piano Series

Piano Progress Studies

Book 1

Graded studies collected and edited by

Fanny Waterman
and
Marion Harewood

Faber Music Limited
London

CONTENTS

This collection © 1986 by Faber Music Ltd
First published in 1986 by Faber Music Ltd
3 Queen Square London WC1N 3AU
Music drawn by Lincoln Castle Music
Cover designed by M & S Tucker
Printed in England by Halstan & Co Ltd
All rights reserved

Staccato and legato

Carl Czerny

Andantino

1

Singing tone

Ferdinand Beyer

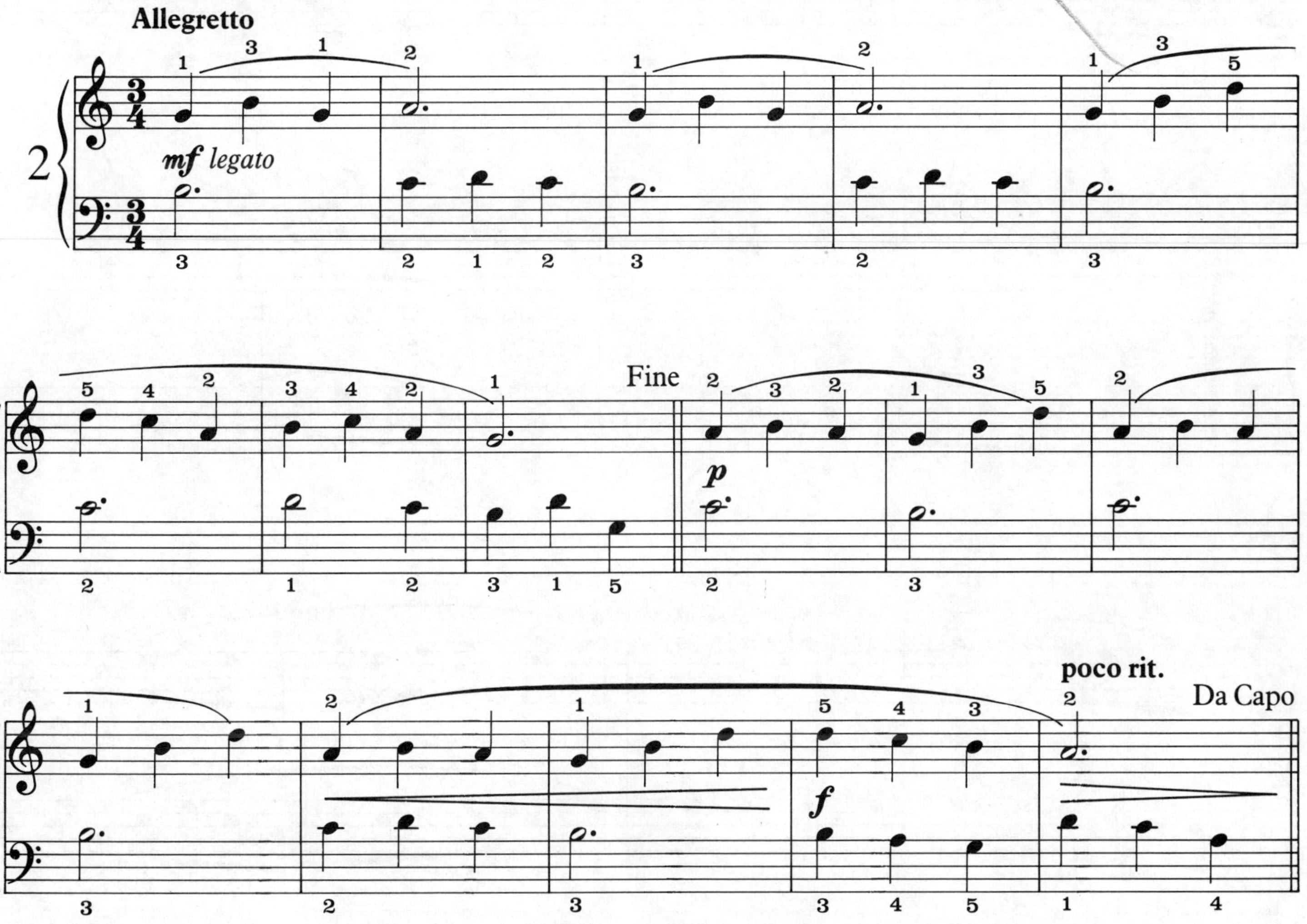

Allegretto

2

Five-finger study

Carl Czerny

Phrasing in both hands

Béla Bartók

4

Shifting positions

Henri Bertini

5

Weak fingers of the right hand

Henri Bertini

Lightness of touch

Carl Czerny

Melodic playing at the octave

Dimitri Kabalevsky

Melody over drone bass

Isidore Philippe

8

Staccato and legato

Carl Czerny

Repeated notes

Zoltán Kodály

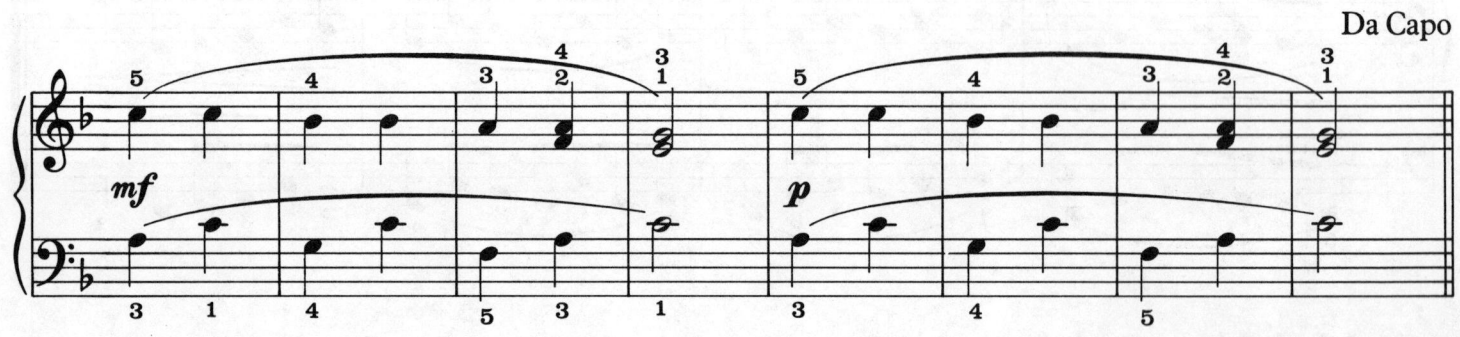

Co-ordination of hands

Daniel Türk

Equality of fingers

August Müller

Melody with accompanying chords

Hermann Berens

Lateral movement (loose wrist)

August Müller

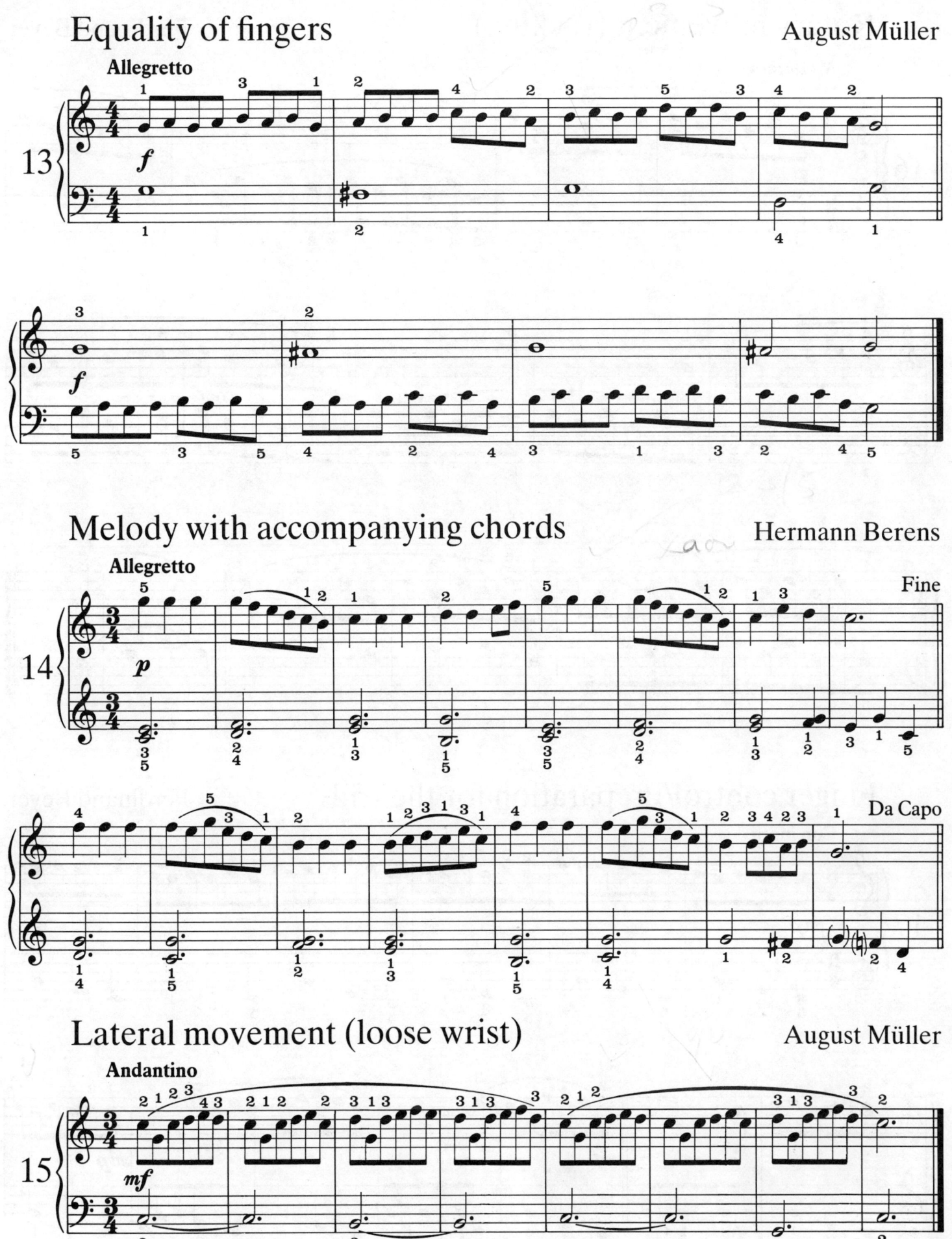

Rotary movement (rocking)

Ferdinand Beyer

Finger control/Preparation for the trill

Ferdinand Beyer

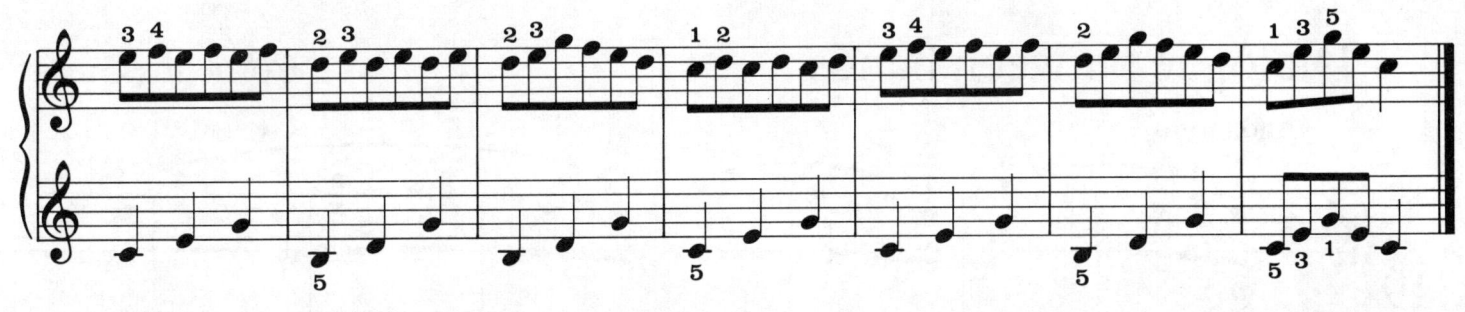

Melody over moving bass

Carl Czerny

Allegretto

p cantabile

18

mf

Dialogue between hands

Cornelius Gurlitt

Double thirds

Ferdinand Beyer

Left-hand singing tone

F. Brunner

21 *Andante*

Legato phrasing

Anton Diabelli

22 *Moderato*

Scale playing

Ferdinand Beyer

23 *Allegro*

[play also in other keys]

Balance between the hands in compound time   Hermann Berens

Couplets and co-ordination   Cornelius Gurlitt

Two voices in close harmony
Daniel Türk

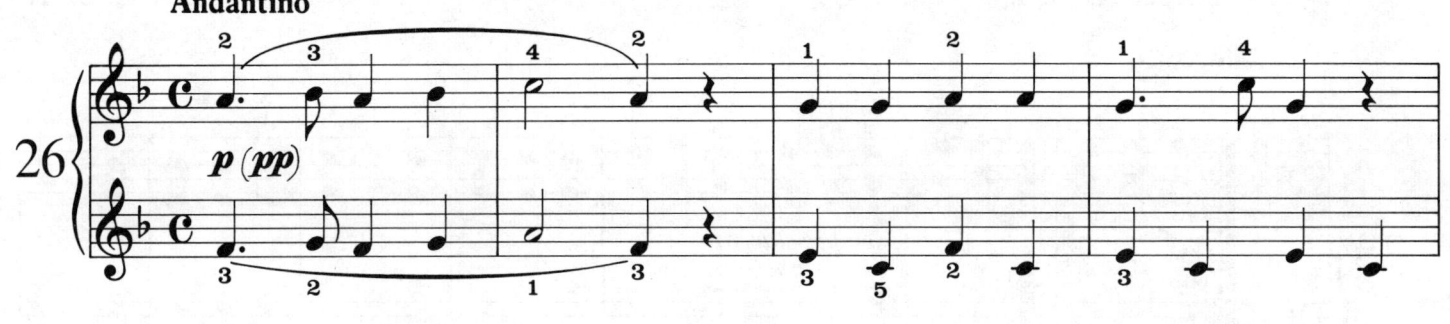

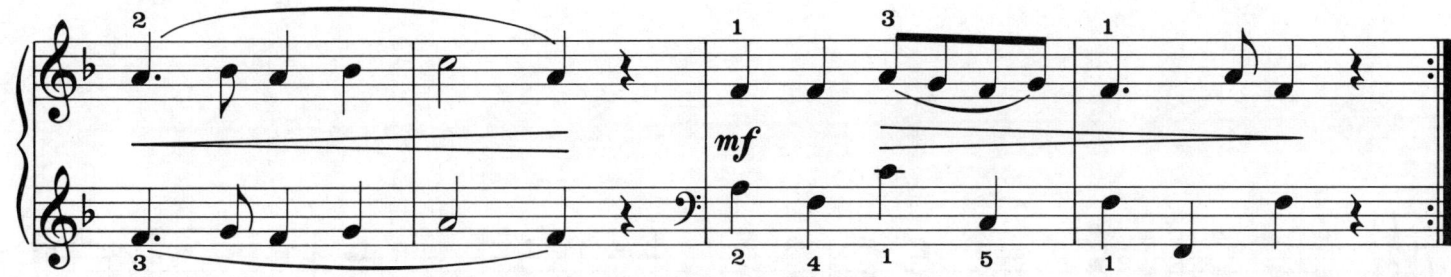

Left-hand chords and Alberti bass
Anton Diabelli

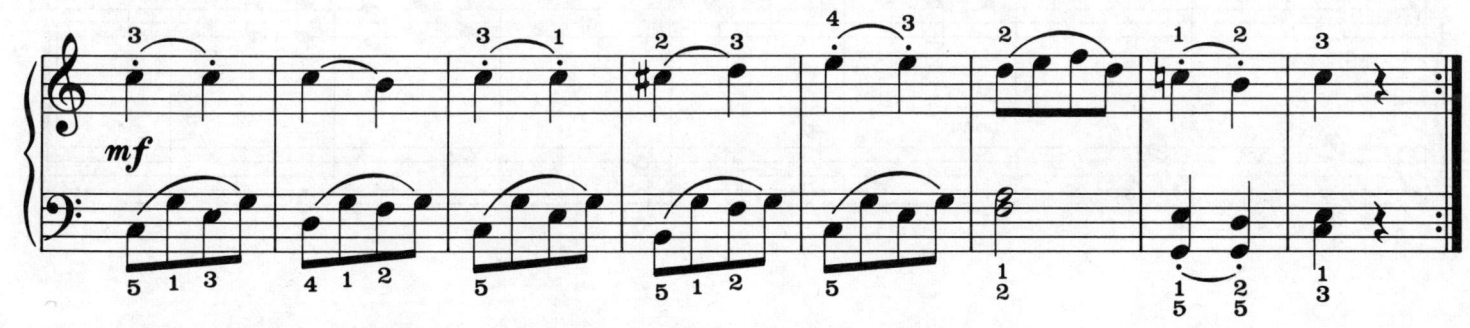

Wrist staccato

Carl Czerny